S0-BAE-907

Historical Biographies

TUTANKHAMEN

Brian Williams

Heinemann Library
Chicago, Illinois

SOUTH HUNTINGTON
PUBLIC LIBRARY
HUNTINGTON STATION, NY 11746

JB
Tutankhamen
w

© 2002 Reed Educational & Professional Publishing
Published by Heinemann Library,
an imprint of Reed Educational & Professional Publishing,
Chicago, Illinois

Customer Service 888-454-2279

Visit our website at www.heinemannlibrary.com

All rights reserved. No part of this publication may be reproduced or transmitted in any form or by any means, electronic or mechanical, including photocopying, recording, taping or any information storage and retrieval system, without permission in writing from the publisher.

Designed by Celia Floyd
Illustrated by Jeff Edwards and Joanna Brooker
Originated by Ambassador Litho Ltd
Printed by Wing King Tong in Hong Kong

06 05 04 03 02
10 9 8 7 6 5 4 3 2 1

Library of Congress Cataloging-in-Publication Data
Williams, Brian, 1959-
   Tutankhamen / Brian Williams.
      p. cm. -- (Historical biographies)
Includes bibliographical references and index.
Summary: Presents an overview of Tutankhamen's life as well as his influence on history and the world.
   ISBN 1-58810-568-7 (HC), 1-4034-0102-0 (Pbk.)
   1. Tutankhamen, King of Egypt--Juvenile literature. 2.
Egypt--History--Eighteenth dynasty, ca. 1320-1200 B.C.--Juvenile
literature. 3. Pharaohs--Biography--Juvenile literature. [1.
Tutankhamen, King of Egypt. 2. Kings, queens, rulers, etc. 3.
Egypt--Civilization--To 332 B.C.] I. Title. II. Series.
   DT87.5 .W5 2002
   932'.014--dc21
                                   2001003663

Acknowledgments

The author and publishers are grateful to the following for permission to reproduce copyright material:

Cover photograph: Corbis

pp. 5, 6, 9, 10, 11, 12, 14, 15, 16, 20, 22, 26, 27 The Art Archive; pp. 7, 8, 18, 21 Corbis; p. 13 Hilary Fletcher; p. 17 Ancient Art and Architecture; pp. 19, 25 Werner Foreman Archive; pp. 23, 24, 28 The Griffiths Institute; p. 29 Hulton Archive.

Special thanks to Rebecca Vickers for her comments in the preparation of this book.

Every effort has been made to contact copyright holders of any material reproduced in this book. Any omissions will be rectified in subsequent printings if notice is given to the publisher.

Some words are shown in bold, **like this.** You can find out what they mean by looking in the glossary.

Many Egyptian names and terms may be found in the pronunciation guide.

30652 00140 3486

Contents

Gift of the Nile

This is the story of Tutankhamen, a **pharaoh** of Egypt, who lived more than 3,000 years ago. Egyptian rulers before Tutankhamen had conquered an empire, and left the biggest **monuments** ever built—the pyramids.

Tutankhamen was not one of these great kings. We know very little about his life, except that it ended before he was twenty years old. However, he is the most famous of all Egyptian kings. His nearly complete **tomb** was discovered by **archaeologist** Howard Carter in 1922. The tomb was full of many amazing objects that help us picture Tutankhamen's life and times. What Carter first saw by flickering candlelight still astonishes museum visitors. Tutankhamen's tomb was like a time capsule, taking us back 3,000 years.

▶ Egypt's rich civilization was made possible by the Nile River. Cities and farms were close to the river. Northern Egypt was called Lower Egypt; the southern part was Upper Egypt.

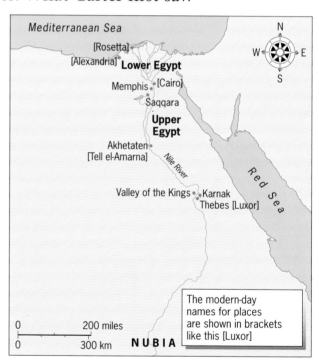

The modern-day names for places are shown in brackets like this [Luxor]

The land of Egypt

Tutankhamen's land was hot and dry, as Egypt still is today. A strip of this desert was made green by the waters of the Nile River, flowing north from the heart of Africa. Every year, the flooding Nile spread dark, fertile soil along its banks, enriching the fields for farmers to grow food.

How do we know?

When Tutankhamen was alive, the pyramids were already over 1,000 years old. Writings on temple walls listed kings dating far back before the pyramids. About 5,000 years ago, King Menes ruled Upper Egypt. He conquered Lower Egypt and united the two kingdoms. Tutankhamen became king about 2,000 years later.

What we know about Tutankhamen comes from the study of the treasures found in his tomb, and from other discoveries. Much is still unclear—who his parents were, for example. Even the dates of Tutankhamen's birth and death are not known for certain.

▶ This is a painted wooden head of Tutankhamen, who became king of Egypt when he was about nine years old. He died about nine years later. The objects buried with him are clues to his life story.

Key dates

3100 B.C.E.	King Menes rules all Egypt
2686–2181 B.C.E.	Great Pyramids built
1333–1323 B.C.E.	Tutankhamen rules Egypt
332 B.C.E.	Egypt conquered by Alexander the Great of Greece
69–30 B.C.E.	Life of Cleopatra, most famous queen of Egypt

Watch the dates

"B.C.E." after a year date means before the common era. This is used instead of the older abbreviation "B.C." The years are counted backwards toward zero. Historians are not sure about the dates of Tutankhamen's **reign**. You may see different dates in different books.

The Sun King's Palace

Tutankhamen was born about 1342 B.C.E. in a new city of temples and palaces. The **pharaoh** Amenhotep IV had moved his entire court 310 miles (500 kilometers) north from the old capital, Thebes, to the building site for his new capital beside the Nile River.

Big changes in Egypt

This king had shocked his people by starting a new religion. He believed in a new sun god, called **Aten**. He had changed his name to Akhenaten, meaning "one useful to Aten."

Egyptians had always worshiped **Amen** and many other gods. Now their king had abandoned the other gods and worshiped only one. Instead of going to war like his father Amenhotep III, he built the beautiful new city he called Akhetaten, "the horizon of Aten." Today, its ruins can be seen at a small town called Tell El-Amarna.

▶ Akhenaten and Queen Nefertiti are shown worshiping the sun god, Aten. Nefertiti shared her husband's new religion.

Pharaoh Akhenaten

Akhenaten ruled Egypt from 1352 to 1336 B.C.E. Sculptures show him with a long, sensitive face and swollen stomach. It is possible he suffered from a **genetic disease**. Akhenaten's favorite wife was Queen Nefertiti. She helped plan their garden-city. The couple had six daughters. They may have been Tutankhamen's half-sisters.

Who were Tutankhamen's parents?

Akhenaten was probably Tutankhamen's father. Some historians think Tutankhamen may have been Akhenaten's younger brother. The Egyptian royal family was complicated because kings often married their sisters and even their daughters. The baby prince was named Tutankhaten, meaning "living image of the Aten." He changed it to Tutankhamen when he became king and restored Egypt's old gods.

Akhenaten had two main wives, Nefertiti and Tutankhamen's mother, Kiya. Kiya may have been a foreign princess. Even so, she was not as important as Nefertiti. She is not mentioned after the eleventh year of Akhenaten's **reign**— maybe she died, perhaps when she gave birth to her son. Without modern medicines, childbirth could be a dangerous time for women. They prayed to the hippo-headed goddess Taweret to protect them.

▶ This stone carving shows Akhenaten and Nefertiti holding hands. Informal art like this was a feature of his reign.

The Little Prince

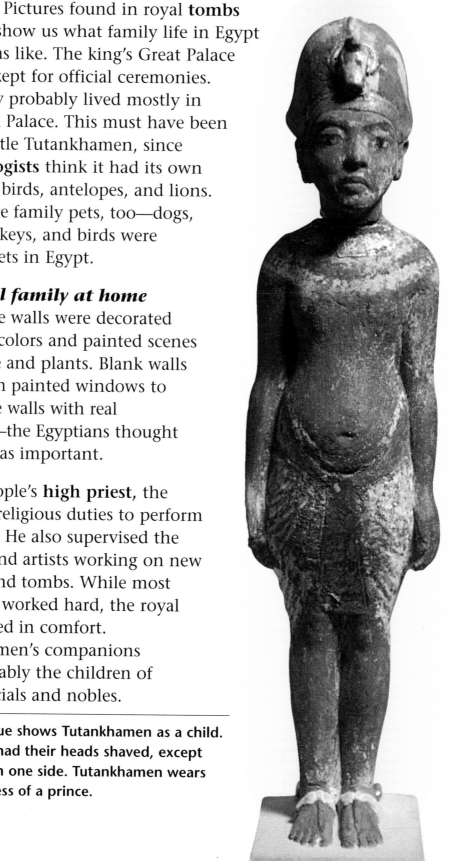

Pictures found in royal **tombs** show us what family life in Egypt was like. The king's Great Palace was kept for official ceremonies. His family probably lived mostly in the North Palace. This must have been fun for little Tutankhamen, since **archaeologists** think it had its own zoo, with birds, antelopes, and lions. There were family pets, too—dogs, cats, monkeys, and birds were favorite pets in Egypt.

The royal family at home

The palace walls were decorated with soft colors and painted scenes of wildlife and plants. Blank walls were given painted windows to match the walls with real windows—the Egyptians thought balance was important.

As the people's **high priest**, the king had religious duties to perform every day. He also supervised the builders and artists working on new temples and tombs. While most Egyptians worked hard, the royal family lived in comfort. Tutankhamen's companions were probably the children of court officials and nobles.

▶ This statue shows Tutankhamen as a child. Boys often had their heads shaved, except for a lock on one side. Tutankhamen wears the headdress of a prince.

Pleasures and sorrows

It must have been fun to be a **pharaoh's** son. Like other princes before him, Tutankhamen paddled boats on the palace lake and caught fish among the water lilies. Sitting in the shade of palm trees, he would have enjoyed his nurse's stories. One popular tale told how a toy crocodile turned into a real one when a naughty child threw it into the water! But for all Egyptians, daily life brought sorrows, too. One of Tutankhamen's sisters, Merykaten, died giving birth to a baby. A tomb picture shows Akhenaten and Nefertiti looking sad, while a nurse holds the baby.

◀ Bes was a popular household god. This bearded dwarf protected children, killed poisonous snakes, and helped the goddess Taweret when babies were being born.

Toys and games

From finds made by archaeologists, we know Egyptian children played with balls (some had seeds inside, so they rattled). They also had pull-along toys, such as toy mice with twitching tails and lions with snapping jaws. Pictures show games of leapfrog and tug-of-war. Four playing-boards for a game called senet were found in Tutankhamen's tomb. In another board game, called snake, players moved counters to get to the snake's head in the middle.

Learning to Rule

Tutankhamen would have been taught to read and write by **scribes.** He had to learn the many picture-signs, or **hieroglyphs,** as well as a new "everyday" writing being encouraged by the king. He was taught history, memorizing the names of the kings who had ruled before him. He also stood beside his father to worship **Aten.**

Lessons

Tutankhamen probably learned family history from Ay, an important government official who was possibly a relative of both the king and Queen Nefertiti. Lessons may have been held in the king's library, full of clay **tablets** and **papyrus scrolls.** There were maps of the empire to look at. Tutankhamen would certainly have learned about the calendar. His year had 365 days, just like ours does.

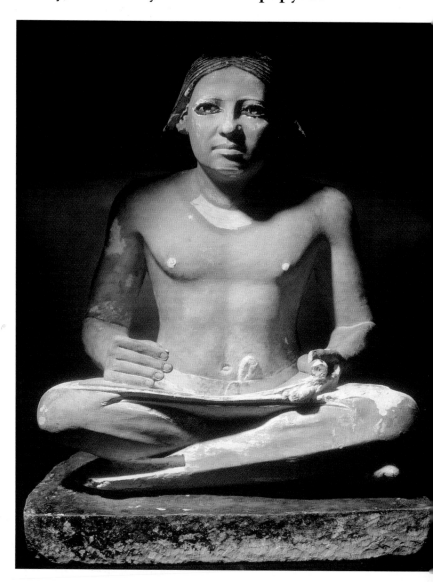

▶ Egyptian scribes wrote on a kind of paper made from the **papyrus reeds** that grew along the banks of the Nile River. They also wrote on soft clay tablets, using pointed sticks.

In Egypt, only boys went to school. Clever boys became priests or scribes, but most poor children started working as soon as they were big enough. Tutankhamen might have crossed the Nile by boat to see farmers growing food in the fields on the far bank. He would have toured the city's grainstores and workshops, and seen the crowded housing for the city workers.

Home life

Small children usually wore no clothes at all. As Tutankhamen grew older his usual clothing would have been a short **kilt** made of **linen**, with reed or leather sandals on his feet. Women of the palace wore long dresses, dyed their hair, and wore makeup and jewelry.

The royal family ate their main meal in the cool of the evening. As they dined, musicians played on harps, flutes, drums, cymbals, and rattles. At feasts, dancers twirled and acrobats tumbled to entertain the king and his guests. On hot nights, people slept on mats on the roof.

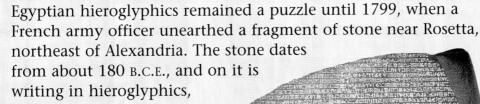

The Rosetta Stone

Egyptian hieroglyphics remained a puzzle until 1799, when a French army officer unearthed a fragment of stone near Rosetta, northeast of Alexandria. The stone dates from about 180 B.C.E., and on it is writing in hieroglyphics, everyday Egyptian writing, and Greek. By comparing the three different scripts, Thomas Young and Jean-François Champollion were able to read hieroglyphs for the first time in the early 1800s.

▶ The Rosetta Stone records the good deeds of Ptolemy V.

The King Is Dead

By the time Tutankhamen was seven, King Akhenaten may already have been ill. It seems he shared power with Smenkhkare, a mystery prince who may have been the king's brother, or a son by another wife (and thus Tutankhamen's half-brother). Some people even think Smenkhkare was Queen Nefertiti, under another name, but this does not seem very likely.

Akhenaten died in about 1336 B.C.E. He was not buried in the Valley of the Kings, the royal burial ground in the desert, but in a secret **tomb.** Smenkhkare also died within two or three years. In 1907, **archaeologists** found a tomb in the Valley of the Kings that may be Smenkhkare's. Tests on bones from a skeleton found in this tomb show that whoever was buried there could have been a brother of Tutankhamen.

▶ Akhenaten was a thinker and art lover, not a soldier like his father, Amenhotep.

▲ The Valley of the Kings lies in the desert on the west side of the Nile River. It is not far from the city of Luxor (ancient Thebes).

Tutankhamen is king

Tutankhamen was now king, though he was only nine years old. Beside him stood the two most powerful men in Egypt, Ay the **counselor** and Horemheb, commander of the army. Waiting in the shadows were the powerful priests of **Amen.** Now they saw their chance to bring back the old gods.

Preparing for death

Egyptians made careful preparations for death and the world they believed that people went to after death. To preserve bodies for this next world, they made **mummies.** Each mummy was placed in a tomb, along with things for the dead person to use in the next world. Some kings were buried in pyramids. Later, kings were buried in rock tombs in the Valley of the Kings. Most tombs were stripped bare by robbers, except for Tutankhamen's. Robbers broke into his tomb, but were chased away before they could take much. That is what makes his tomb so important to **archaeologists.**

The New King Reigns

Although he was only nine, the new king was married at once. The Egyptians believed it was important that a king be married to a person of equal rank. The wife chosen for Tutankhamen was Ankhesenpaten. She was the third of Akhenaten's six daughters with Nefertiti, and therefore possibly Tutankhamen's half-sister.

The old ways return

Although Tutankhamen **reigned**, he was too young to rule. He did what his advisers told him. He still worshiped **Aten** in his father's city, but in the second year of his reign, he gave up his old name of Tutankhaten. His wife also replaced the *aten* part of her name with *amen*.

Tutankhamen was not crowned king at once. His coronation by the high priests of **Amen** took place about three years later. He was crowned at the temple of Karnak, the main center for worship of Amen. After this, he lived in palaces at nearby Thebes (once again Egypt's capital) and at Memphis.

▶ Cartouches were oval frames around the names of kings, queens, and gods. This picture shows Tutankhamen's cartouche on the side of a **canopic** box.

A boy and his treasures

Too small for the royal throne, the boy-king probably still sat on a child's chair. Several chairs were buried with him. Artists brought him wonderful treasures, such as beautiful gold jewelry set with blue and red gemstones from the desert. Perhaps, though, he treasured family memories most. In his **tomb** were later placed an artist's palette belonging to his sister Merykaten, and the lid of a box with a picture of another sister.

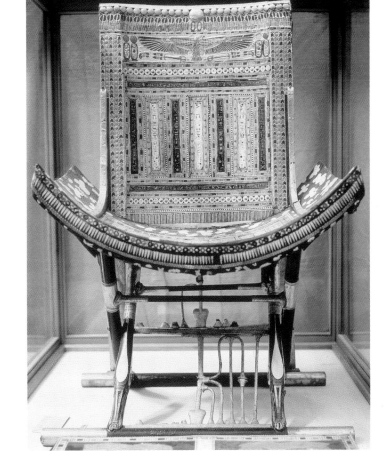

► This chair is so richly decorated with ebony, **ivory,** and gold that it is called a throne—but it is really a folding stool. On it are the names Tutankhaten and Tutankhamen.

Royal marriages

Marrying a daughter or a sister is not allowed by law now, but the Egyptians thought it made the king more like a god. Had Tutankhamen lived longer, he would probably have married other wives—a foreign princess, perhaps, or a **commoner.** Queen Tiy, wife of Amenhotep III, had been an important soldier's daughter.

Lord of All

Tutankhamen probably wanted to see for himself the land of which he was lord and master. The best way to travel was by boat along the Nile. The king would have been escorted by other boats carrying servants, guards, musicians, tents, food, and drink. Belongings were packed in sacks, baskets, and chests fastened with wooden locks or rope bindings. Horses and **chariots** followed along the shore. At night, the royal party probably camped beside the river.

Life on the Nile

There was much to see—people fishing, farmers using **shadufs** to tip river water into ditches to water crops, boats laden with grain and vegetables, and barges weighed down by blocks of building stone. In the shallows, men washed clothes, always keeping a watchful eye open for crocodiles.

▶ Hunters in this **tomb** painting throw weighted sticks to catch wild ducks. Villagers kept tame ducks and geese for eggs. There were no chickens in Egypt.

Egyptian boats

Thirty-five miniature boats were found in Tutankhamen's tomb. Wood was scarce, so small boats were made from bundles of **papyrus reeds** bound together with ropes. The king's riverboat was as big as the ships that traded across the Mediterranean and Red Seas.

A hunting trip

The handle of a fan found in Tutankhamen's tomb pictures the king hunting ostriches. Writing on the handle tells us that the feathers for the fan were collected during a royal hunt. Hunting was a favorite sport in Egypt. It is likely that Tutankhamen would have gone hunting in the desert with his soldier friends. As a boy, he would have been taught to drive a chariot and to shoot a bow, other items found in his tomb. As king, he could pick the fastest horses, and his favorite hounds would have raced beside his chariot.

After the hunt, the royal party probably feasted on roast ostrich. Stretched on a camp bed in his tent, the young king doubtless felt content to be lord of all.

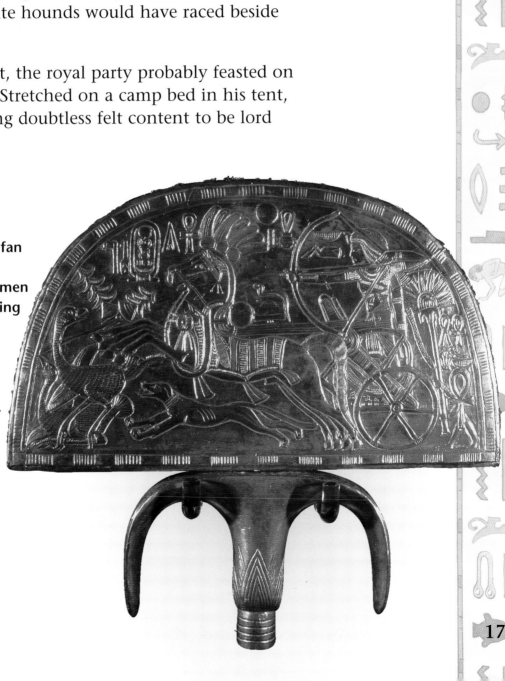

▶ On this gold fan handle from his tomb, Tutankhamen is pictured hunting ostriches. The ostrich feathers on the fan had been eaten away by insects.

The Might of Egypt

As **pharaoh**, Tutankhamen was commander-in-chief of Egypt's army. Kings sometimes led armies into battle, riding in war **chariots**. Pictures of these warlike kings with defeated prisoners reminded everyone of past glories. The young Tutankhamen would have been told of enemies, such as the **Hittites**.

The king's army

The Egyptian army had many foot soldiers. Soldiers were armed with **bronze** daggers and short swords, axes, and clubs. They carried shields made of tough, dried ox-skin. Spearmen threw long spears tipped with copper or bronze points, and archers fired double-curved bows. The Egyptians had learned how to use these bows from their old enemies, the Hyksos, and some could shoot arrows up to 1,300 feet (400 meters). They rode into battle on horse-drawn chariots, fired into the enemy ranks, then raced away.

General Horemheb led an army north into Lebanon and Palestine to fight the Hittites. He also fought against the **Nubians** in the south, where Egypt was once again victorious. **Tomb** pictures show that Tutankhamen got the glory for these victories, but he probably never left Egypt himself.

▶ This wooden figure shows Tutankhamen with a harpoon, as if about to spear a Nile hippopotamus. It was made for a religious ceremony.

Tribute from afar

One of Tutankhamen's officials was Huy, his governor in Nubia. In Huy's tomb, there is a huge painting of him presenting visiting princes of Nubia to the boy-king. The Nubians brought rich gifts as **tribute**, including wild animals for the royal zoo.

▲ The giraffe on this tomb painting is a tribute to the pharaoh. The foreigners offering it may be Nubians from the south.

Stronger weapons

Although they were such an advanced people, the Egyptians were slow to use iron. The Hittites were the first to make iron swords and spears. Egyptian soldiers still used copper or bronze weapons, that could easily snap. A rare iron dagger was found in Tutankhamen's tomb.

Temple-builder

When Tutankhamen came to power, he restored the old religion. Every morning, the young **pharaoh** went to the **temple** to start the day. Priests again wore leopard-skin cloaks (hidden away during Akhenaten's **reign**). Two cloaks—one of real leopard skin, one of cloth—were found in Tutankhamen's **tomb**.

Return of the old gods

Ay, Tutankhamen's **counselor**, encouraged this return to the old gods **Amen**, Re, and Ptah. All three gods are shown on a trumpet found in Tutankhamen's tomb. A wooden statue of Ptah, the chief god of the old city of Memphis, was buried with Tutankhamen.

In official writings, the great Amenhotep III was now called Tutankhamen's "father." The new city of Akhetaten was abandoned. It was as if Akhenaten had never existed.

▲ This **papyrus scroll** shows what people believed happened after death. First, the jackal-headed god Anubis weighed the soul of a dead person against the ostrich feather of Ma'at, goddess of truth. The god Osiris then decided the fate of the soul.

▼ Wooden and **bronze** tools including an adze for shaping wood were used in temple-building around the time of Tutankhamen.

Building temples and tombs

New temples were built and old ones repaired. Many of the workers were prisoners of war. Massive blocks of stone were shipped along the Nile by barge, and then dragged overland on sledges. This is how the pyramids had been built over 1,000 years earlier.

Treasurer Maya was the official in charge of the "Place of Eternity," the Valley of the Kings. In this dry valley were the rock tombs of the pharaohs. Tutankhamen would one day join them, but work on his royal tomb had not yet begun.

Egyptian tools

Metal tools were so valuable that workers had to return them to the site storeroom at the end of the day. The tools were weighed on balance scales in the morning and in the evening, to make sure that crafty workers were not chipping off bits of metal to melt down and sell.

The Nile Floods

To Egyptians, the Nile was simply "the river." Every year in July, the waters of the Nile began to rise, swollen by heavy rains in the tropical heart of Africa. The people rejoiced. This flood was welcomed, not feared. Without it, there would be no crops, no food, no life in Egypt.

The king led the ceremony of thanksgiving. He praised the gods for bringing new life to the land and asked for a rich harvest. The black soil was turned by wooden plows pulled by oxen. This dark soil gave Egypt its name—Kemet, "the black land."

Farming in Egypt

Farmers either owned or rented small farms that belonged to large estates, held by the king. Government officials visited every farm twice a year, first to count fields and animals, and later to collect part of the harvest. This gathered food went to feed the rest of Egypt's workers.

▶ The top picture shows Egyptian farmers making haystacks at harvesttime. The grain stalks were cut with sickles edged with sharp flints. Below, grains are separated from stalks by pulling them through combs.

The most important crops were wheat, used to make flour for bread-making, and barley, for brewing beer. Flax was also grown to make **linen**. Dates, a favorite dessert, were harvested in August. They were dried in the sun to preserve them. Dates and grapes were made into wine. Honey collected from beehives was used to sweeten foods.

Thanking the river god

When the harvest was gathered, Tutankhamen and his queen gave thanks to the river god, Hapi. The **pharaoh** offered gifts of food, ornaments, and jewels to the god's statue.

▲ The oval wooden boxes found in Tutankhamen's **tomb** held meat for him to eat.

Food in Egypt

In the palace, people dined on beef, lamb, and wild antelope. Poor people did not eat meat often. They ate mainly bread and vegetables, with fish or birds as a treat. Egyptians grew beans, lentils, lettuce, onions, leeks, melons, cucumbers, and pomegranates. They loved figs—but so did wild baboons, who were often chased away by farmers! In Tutankhamen's tomb, there were 116 baskets of food and 30 jars of wine.

A Brief Reign Ends

Pictures of Tutankhamen and his queen show a happy couple, but this happiness was short-lived. Tutankhamen prayed for a son to succeed him as ruler. Twice the queen was pregnant, but each time the babies were born dead. The king and queen grieved as the tiny bodies were **mummified.** The babies were later buried with their father.

In about 1323 B.C.E., Tutankhamen died. The exact date is not known, and how he died is a mystery. Examination of his mummy found no proof that he was weak or ill. He was slim, about five feet, five inches (1.65 meters) tall, and his bones and teeth show that he was seventeen or eighteen years old. X-rays did reveal a tiny piece of bone chipped from his skull. He may have fallen from his **chariot.** It is also possible that he was murdered.

Becoming a mummy

After his death, the young king was handed over to **embalmers** for mummification. This process took 70 days. The embalmers removed the brain, stomach, liver, and intestines. Usually, these organs were put into **canopic** jars, but Tutankhamen's were buried in four miniature **coffins.** The heart remained in the body.

▶ This is Tutankhamen's mummy. Only one royal mummy had been found in its **tomb** before. The body inside the decayed **linen** wrappings was poorly preserved.

The body was treated with salts, and packed with linen, sawdust, or dry **lichen.** Painted stone eyes were placed in the eye sockets. The body was rubbed with lotions and oils, and then wrapped in cloth. The dead king's fingers and toes were individually bandaged, and a gold mask was made to cover his face.

Furniture, treasures, food, and other items were collected to go into the dead king's tomb. All was then ready for the funeral.

▲ Tutankhamen's **shrine** was decorated with scenes. Some of these scenes show him and his queen together. In this scene, the king pours water into the queen's cupped hand.

Furniture

Furniture put into Tutankhamen's tomb included lamps, jars, chests, beds, and chairs. Royal furniture was much grander than the simple wooden tables and stools in poor people's homes. The king's small chair was made of ebony wood, imported from Africa. There were eight beds in the tomb—one a folding camp bed—and four headrests, one made of **ivory.** Egyptians used headrests instead of pillows.

Buried and Forgotten

Tutankhamen's **mummy** was taken across the Nile by boat to the Valley of the Kings. No royal **tomb** was ready, so he was buried in a small tomb, maybe intended for Ay. On the tomb walls are paintings showing the young king's welcome by the gods.

A vast crowd probably watched the funeral procession, as the king's mummy was carried into the tomb, but only eight people attended the funeral banquet. The flower-collar, or wreath, worn by one of them was to be a vital clue to rediscovering Tutankhamen's tomb.

▲ In this painting from the burial chamber, Ay (on the right) performs the "Opening of the Mouth" ceremony on Tutankhamen to prepare him for the afterlife.

What happened next

After Tutankhamen's death, his queen needed to remarry. She wrote to the **Hittite** king seeking a husband. A Hittite prince came to Egypt, but he was murdered at once—probably on the orders of General Horemheb. Queen Ankhesenpaten had to marry the aging Ay, who then became the new king.

Tutankhamen's tomb was closed, but robbers broke in at least twice, stealing some jewelry and other items. One thief left his footprint on a white box, still visible 3,000 years later. **Treasurer** Maya acted swiftly to close the tomb up again. Perhaps he guarded it for the rest of his life.

Tutankhamen vanishes from history

Ay ruled Egypt for only four years. When the old man died, he was buried in a new tomb, probably one meant for Tutankhamen. Horemheb made himself **pharaoh** and tried to destroy all traces of the past. Ay's tomb was smashed. Tutankhamen's name was scratched off **monuments.** The **temple** of **Aten** was destroyed. The boy-king's tomb was hidden by rubble, and soon both the tomb and Tutankhamen himself were forgotten.

▲ Tutankhamen was buried in three **coffins,** one inside the other. The two outer ones were wood, richly decorated with gold. The innermost coffin weighed 240 pounds (110 kilograms) and was made of solid gold. This painting on the tomb wall shows the king being welcomed by a goddess.

The mummy hunters

Foreigners began visiting the Valley of the Kings 2,000 years ago, when Roman tourists inspected empty tombs. Some mummies were sold as curiosities, but the Egyptians hid many of the royal mummies. When Howard Carter opened Tutankhamen's tomb, 33 royal tombs were known in the Valley of the Kings, but all had been robbed long ago. More tombs have since been found.

27

Wonders Revealed

In 1907, an American named Theodore Davis was **excavating** in the Valley of the Kings. His team found a cup with Tutankhamen's name on it, some scraps of gold foil with pictures of the **pharaoh**, and pottery jars left over from a funeral. In one jar were faded floral collars. Could these be clues to finding a lost **tomb?**

Howard Carter, a British **archaeologist** working for a rich aristocrat named Lord Carnarvon, took up the search. In 1914, Carter began looking for Tutankhamen's tomb. In 1922, while clearing away rubble left by the tomb builders for a later king named Ramses VI, he found steps leading down to a door. It was the entrance to a tomb, still closed up. It had not been opened for 3,000 years.

Inside the tomb

When Carter opened the tomb, he saw "wonderful things." The tomb itself was fairly small. Within a golden **shrine**, in a **sarcophagus**, were three **coffins.** Finally, beneath the wrappings and the gold funeral mask, the **mummy** was revealed.

▶ Many of the precious items found in the tomb had been piled up hastily when it was closed up again after the robberies. Fortunately, the robbers had not returned.

Tutankhamen was not a great king, yet his tomb treasures are the richest so far recovered from an Egyptian royal tomb. By studying them, historians have learned much more about life in ancient Egypt. Finding Tutankhamen's tomb was a thrilling story of historical detective work, turning the forgotten boy-king into the most famous pharaoh of them all.

▶ **Howard Carter opened the burial chamber on February 17, 1923. Hundreds of excited people waited to hear what he had found. He chipped a small hole and shone a torch inside to see "an astonishing sight...a solid wall of gold." It was Tutankhamen's gold-coated shrine.**

Tutankhamen's treasures

Tutankhamen's treasures are displayed in the Egyptian Museum in Cairo, the capital of Egypt. Many of the objects are very delicate. Wood brought out of the tomb into the dry dessert air began to crack and shrink. Cloth and leather had rotted away, as had the threads of necklaces. Howard Carter made careful drawings of many objects, while Harry Burton took photographs. They put a number on each item to record exactly where it was found.

Glossary

Amen one of the most important gods in Egypt; also spelled Amun and Amon

archaeologist person who finds out about the past by studying the remains of buildings and other objects

Aten Egyptian sun god

bronze metal made by mixing melted copper and tin

canopic relating to decorated jars or boxes of wood, stone, or clay, in which Egyptians put the four "vital organs" of a dead person

chariot light cart with two wheels, pulled by horses

coffin box in which the body of a dead person is put

commoner person who is not an aristocrat or noble

counselor person who gives advice

embalmer person who preserves a dead body as a mummy

excavating digging into the ground by archaeologists to uncover the ruins of a building or a tomb

genetic disease illness that is passed on from parents to children

hieroglyph character in Egyptian picture-writing. The name means "sacred writing" in Greek.

high priest senior or most important priest

Hittite one of an ancient, warlike people who lived in what is now Turkey

ivory hard, white material of an elephant's tusks

kilt skirtlike garment

lichen small, dry plant growing on rocks and trees

linen cloth made from the woven fibers of the flax plant

monument building or statue built to remind people of a famous person or a famous event

mummy body of a dead person that has been specially treated to keep it from decaying

Nubian person from an area to the south of Egypt, in what is now Sudan, that was once part of the Egyptian empire

papyrus reed used to make paper

papyrus scroll Egyptian book made from a long strip of papyrus-reed paper wrapped in a roll around a stick

pharaoh ruler of Egypt

reed tall plant growing beside rivers and lakes

reign time during which a king or queen rules

sarcophagus stone coffin, often with other coffins inside it

scribe person trained to write. They often wrote government records and letters for other people.

shaduf simple machine for lifting water, using a long pole with a weight at one end and a bucket at the other

shrine especially holy place, or a container with doors, inside which a god's statue or a royal coffin was kept

tablet small, flat piece of clay or stone used for writing on

temple building in which people worship a god or gods

tomb burial place, often marked by a stone or building

treasurer government official in charge of money, including spending it and collecting taxes

tribute gift given to a ruler by people, often paid as a kind of tax

Time Line

3100 B.C.E.	King Menes, the first **pharaoh**, rules all Egypt
2686–2181 B.C.E.	Imhotep builds the first pyramid at Saqqara. King Khufu builds the Great Pyramid at Giza.
2040–1786 B.C.E.	First schools in Egypt. **Amen** of Thebes becomes an important god. City of Thebes becomes the capital.
1390–1353 B.C.E.	**Reign** of Amenhotep III
1352–1336 B.C.E.	Reign of Akhenaten
1335–1333 B.C.E.	Reign of Smenkhkare
1333–1323 B.C.E.	Tutankhamen rules Egypt
332 B.C.E.	Alexander the Great conquers Egypt. He makes Alexandria the capital. Greek kings known as Ptolemies rule Egypt.
69–30 B.C.E.	Life of Cleopatra, Queen of Egypt from 51 B.C.E. After her death, Egypt is ruled by Rome.

Pronunciation Guide

Word	You say
Akhenaten	ah-ke-NAH-ten
Akhetaten	ah-ke-TAH-ten
Amenhotep	ah-men-HOE-tep
canopic	ka-NO-pic
cartouche	car-TOOSH
hieroglyph	HIGH-ro-glif
Osiris	oh-SIGH-ris
Ptolemy	TAH-le-mee
shaduf	sha-DOOF
Tutankhamen	toot-ahngk-AH-men

More Books to Read

MacDonald, Fiona. *The World in the Time of Tutankhamen.* Broomall, Penn.: Chelsea House, 2000. An older reader can help you with this book.

Pemberton, Delia. *Egyptian Mummies: People from the Past.* Orlando, Fla.: Harcourt Children's Books, 2001.

Shuter, Jane. *The Ancient Egyptians.* Chicago: Heinemann Library, 1997.

Index

DISCARDED

JB TUTANKHAMEN   W
Williams, Brian
Tutankhamen

$22.79

DATE			

DEC 15 2003

**SOUTH HUNTINGTON
PUBLIC LIBRARY**
HUNTINGTON STATION, NY 11746.

BAKER & TAYLOR